A Day at the Beach
Animal Life on the Shore

Seagulls

by Ellen Lawrence

Consultant:

Julie Ellis
Research Assistant Professor
Cummings School of Veterinary Medicine
Tufts University
North Grafton, Massachusetts

BEARPORT PUBLISHING

New York, New York

Credits

Cover, © Daan Schoonhooven/Minden Pictures/FLPA, © Vyacheslav Pokrovskiy/Shutterstock, and © littlewormy/Shutterstock; 2, © GlobalIP/iStock; 4, © Jeff Carpenter/Shutterstock; 5T, © Evlakhov Valeriy/Shutterstock; 5B, © David Tipling/FLPA; 6, © Dirk M. de Boer/Shutterstock; 7, © Abi Warner/Shutterstock; 8, © Maciej Olszewski/Shutterstock; 9, © Dalibor Danilovic/Shutterstock; 10T, © Cheryl Ann Quigley/Shutterstock; 10C, © bonchan/Shutterstock; 10BL, © Hong Vo/Shutterstock; 10BR, © IDI974/Shutterstock; 11, © Jeff Smith/Perspectives/Shutterstock; 12, © Maciej Olszewski/Shutterstock; 13, © Dominique Halleux/Biosphoto; 14, © Robert Royse, BIA/Minden Pictures/FLPA; 15, © Pete Oxford/Minden Pictures/FLPA; 16, © Design Pics Inc/Alamy; 17, © Sanchezn/Wikimedia Commons; 18, © BMJ/Shutterstock; 19, © Nik Taylor Wildlife/Alamy; 20T, © Cristian Gusa/Shutterstock; 20B, © Dirk M. de Boer/Shutterstock; 21, © Peter Elvidge/Shutterstock; 22L, © Klaus Rassinger and Gerhard Cammerer/Museum Wiesbaden; 22TR, © Pascale Gueret/Shutterstock; 22BR, © Shotshop GmbH/Alamy; 23TL, © Brian E. Kushner/Shutterstock; 23TC, © Ian Dyball/Shutterstock; 23TR, © Sylvie Bouchard/Shutterstock; 23BL, © Brian E. Kushner/Shutterstock; 23BC, © Abdulzhelilova Susan/Shutterstock; 23BR, © Christian Musat/Shutterstock.

Publisher: Kenn Goin
Senior Editor: Joyce Tavolacci
Creative Director: Spencer Brinker
Photo Researcher: Ruth Owen Books

Library of Congress Cataloging-in-Publication Data

Names: Lawrence, Ellen, 1967– author.
Title: Seagulls / by Ellen Lawrence.
Description: New York, N.Y. : Bearport Publishing, [2018] | Series: A day at the beach: Animal life on the shore | Includes bibliographical references and index.
Identifiers: LCCN 2017048990 (print) | LCCN 2017049604 (ebook) |
ISBN 9781684025053 (ebook) | ISBN 9781684024476 (library)
Subjects: LCSH: Gulls—Juvenile literature.
Classification: LCC QL696.C46 (ebook) | LCC QL696.C46 L39 2018 (print) | DDC 598.3/38—dc23
LC record available at https://lccn.loc.gov/2017048990

For more information, write to Bearport Publishing Company, Inc., 45 West 21st Street, Suite 3B, New York, New York 10010. Printed in the United States of America.

10 9 8 7 6 5 4 3 2 1

Contents

A Fishy Feast

A fishing boat is chugging toward the seashore.

It's chased by squawking seagulls.

The birds know that fishers throw fish guts and other scraps overboard.

The birds swoop down to gobble up the food.

When their fishy feast is over, they fly back to the beach to rest.

seagulls fighting over a fish

The birds known as seagulls are actually herring gulls. They are named after a type of fish, even though they eat lots of different foods.

herring

All About Herring Gulls

Herring gulls, or seagulls, are large seabirds with gray and white feathers.

An adult gull weighs about 2.5 pounds (1.1 kg).

Its wings can measure more than 4 feet (1.2 m) across!

Seagulls spend their days looking for food, bathing in the sea, and resting on rocks.

adult herring gull

a drop of salty snot

If there is no freshwater around, seagulls can drink salty seawater. Too much salt is bad for the birds, but their bodies are able to remove it. The salt drips from the gulls' nostrils as salty snot!

7

A Seagull's World

Seagulls are found in many places around the world.

They live in almost every part of North America.

Hundreds of seagulls may gather together on beaches or rocky cliffs.

Other seagulls live far from the sea but still near water.

They make their homes close to rivers or lakes.

seagulls on a cliff

What foods do you think a seagull might eat at the seashore?

Some seagulls spend time at landfills, where there's lots of trash. They feed on leftover food they find in the garbage.

seagulls at a landfill

9

Gull Grub

Seagulls will eat just about anything!

They dive into the ocean to catch fish.

They also look for food in shallow water and tide pools.

There, they feed on starfish, sea urchins, and **shellfish**, such as crabs and whelks.

Sometimes, seagulls eat smaller birds and their eggs.

starfish

whelk

sea urchin

crab

10

Seagulls are **scavengers** that eat dead animals. They also raid trash cans on beaches to find food. Sometimes, they'll snatch food right out of a person's hand!

How do you think a seagull breaks open the hard shell of a crab, whelk, or other shellfish?
(The answer is on page 24.)

11

Bird Talk

When a seagull becomes an adult, it finds a **mate**.

Each pair of birds chooses a **territory**.

If a neighbor comes into its territory, a gull gives a long screeching call that means "Go away!"

If that doesn't work, the gull makes a mewing sound to call its mate.

This sound means "Help me scare away this **intruder**!"

a gull giving a "Go away!" call

12

a pair of gulls sharing food

A seagull pair's territory measures about 16 feet by 16 feet (5 m by 5 m). That's about the size of a large room.

Building a Nest

A pair of seagulls chooses a place in their territory for a nest.

They build it using plants and trash, including bits of rope and fishing nets.

There, the female gull lays up to three large, speckled eggs.

Then she sits on the eggs to keep them warm.

After about 32 days, chicks hatch from the eggs.

nest

As the seagull pair looks for a place to build a nest, they make *Huoh, Huoh, Huoh* noises to each other. The birds point to different places with their beaks. Then they choose their favorite nesting spot.

Splat Attack!

The tiny seagull chicks are in danger from eagles, foxes, and other **predators**.

If an enemy comes close, the parent birds give a loud warning cry.

Any gulls that are nearby come to help scare away the animal.

The gulls dive at the predator, whacking it with their bodies.

They will also peck at the attacker until it goes away.

red spot

A parent seagull has a red spot on its beak. How do you think the spot is helpful to its chicks?

poop

Seagulls also have some unusual ways to scare away predators. They squirt the animal with stinky poop and even vomit on the attacker!

Hungry Chicks

At first, the parent seagulls take turns finding food for the chicks.

When a parent bird returns to the nest with food, the chicks tap a red spot on its beak.

This action tells the adult that the babies are ready to eat.

After about four weeks, both parents leave the nest to look for food for their growing chicks.

one-week-old chick

12-week-old chick

adult seagull

At about 12 weeks old, the chicks are the same size as their parents.

dead fish

Growing Up

The seagull chicks stay with their parents until they're about three months old.

Then it's time for the chicks to take care of themselves.

As a young gull grows up, its feathers change color.

It doesn't become a fully gray and white adult until it's four years old.

Then the seagull is ready to find a mate and have chicks of its own!

10-month-old seagull

3-year-old seagull

Once a seagull has found a mate, the birds will often stay together for several years. A seagull can live for more than 20 years.

Science Lab

Be a Seagull Scientist!

We know a lot about seagulls because scientists have studied them for many years. Now it's your turn to investigate! Read the following questions and write your answers in a notebook.

I. This seagull egg is life-size. Use a ruler to measure the egg's size. Then measure a chicken's egg. Is the gull egg bigger or smaller than a chicken's egg?

2. Why do you think a seagull chick has gray, speckled feathers?

3. What do you think the seagull on the left is doing in this picture?

(The answers are on page 24.)

Science Words

intruder (in-TROOD-uhr) an animal that enters a place forcefully

mate (MAYT) an animal's partner with which it has babies

predators (PRED-uh-turz) animals that hunt other animals for food

scavengers (SKAV-uhn-juhrz) animals that feed on the dead bodies of other animals

shellfish (SHEL-fish) ocean animals with a shell, such as crabs, mussels, or shrimp

territory (TER-uh-tor-ee) the area where an animal lives, finds food, and raises its young

Index

Read More

Metz, Lorijo. *Discovering Seagulls (Along the Shore).* New York: Rosen (2011).

Owen, Ruth. *Welcome to the Seashore (Nature's Neighborhoods: All About Ecosystems).* New York: Ruby Tuesday Books (2016).

Wilkins, John-Paul. *What Can Live at the Beach? (What Can Live There?).* Mankato, MN: Heinemann (2014).

Learn More Online

To learn more about seagulls, visit **www.bearportpublishing.com/ ADayAtTheBeach**

About the Author

Ellen Lawrence lives in the United Kingdom. Her favorite books to write are those about nature and animals. In fact, the first book Ellen bought for herself when she was six years old was the story of a gorilla named Patty Cake that was born in New York's Central Park Zoo.

Answers

Page 11: A seagull uses its powerful beak to break open an animal's shell. It might also drop the animal onto a rock, so its shell cracks open.

Page 22:

1. The egg is 3 inches (7.6 cm) long. It's bigger than a chicken's egg.

2. A chick has speckled feathers to help it blend in with rocks or sand and hide from predators.

3. The seagull on the left is giving a long, loud call to tell the other bird to stay out of its territory.